Places

Robert
Creeley

The lunatic, the lover, and the poet
Are of imagination all compact.
One sees more devils than vast hell can hold:
That is the madman. The lover, all as frantic,
Sees Helen's beauty in the brow of Egypt.
The poet's eye, in a fine frenzy rolling,
Doth glance from heaven to earth, from earth to heaven;
And as imagination bodies forth
The forms of things unknown, the poet's pen
Turns them to shapes, and gives to airy nothing
A local habitation and a name.

A Midsummer Night's Dream, V.i.7-17

Local Habitations

Writing from Buffalo

Robert Creeley, **Places**
John Clarke, **In the Analogy**
David Tirrell, **The Half-House Poems**
Elizabeth Willis, **A/O**
Marten Clibbens, **Torch**
Lisa Jarnot, **The Fall of Orpheus**
Randy Prus, **Ice**
Sheryl Robbins, **Queen of the Dead Lakes**
Bruce Holsapple, **Observations**
Mike Boughn, **Geographemes**

Places

Places

Robert
Creeley

Paintings by Susan Barnes

Shuffaloff press

415 Norwood Ave.
Buffalo, N.Y. 14222

for Jack & Cass
con amore

"Places everybody..."

"As a Young/Man..."

for Jean Daive

As a young
man I walked
the streets

of Paris with
infant sons, dis-
placed wife, we

visited an
American married
to a Frenchwoman

at her family's
flat in the
suburbs and

were driven back
to our meager
digs in a Citroen

I recall. Now
old, what else do
I remember of

that city? Much
more—an evening,
years later, rather

a night, late,
I'd come back to
the pension off

the Place Vendome,
my room an edge
of building some

three floors up,
undressed, then, on
impulse, stepped

out, naked, onto
small balcony into
fresh summer's night.

As If

Not the sight
of sea blue with
sudden gull but
the glasses it's
seen through as
life like as
ever it was.

Don & Linda's House

Place, light,
windows look
in, look out—

pots, plants,
green ground,
roses, the flowers
abound—

This archaic
language feels
the insistence,
the common ground.

—Jerusalem, April 30, 1989

Dogs

Dogs face off
in way makes me envious.

Could one so stare down
imagined enemy—

kick the dirt around,
piss on the ground.

For Debora

"I have forgotten all
human relations, but not

poetry." I have for-
gotten all that seemed

significant but not
the consequence I have

never seen this before
this I have wanted to

make this trip many
times but got lost getting

there I have had many
sorrows in my literal

life but much happiness
also I have forgotten

what it was they thought
to remember. I have forgotten.

Hotel

Photo of kid on desk in
abstract place is face of
person how old now
and where and when
did he or will
he leave now, come
back to say hello.

"I Know This..."

I know this
silence despite the
under-roar of the cars
on the roads below.

Air still blows over
it, blows it away, bird's
seemingly shy, testing
whistle, a closer sound.

Horn squawk, squeal
of familar brakes, some
higher sound, and tires
all groan with their load.

You think God's up
there, looking down?
He must be some-
where, maybe taking

a walk on the comforting
earth, or just lets
these various breezes
ruffle that ancient hair.

The Kinderspielplatz/Halensee Park

Empty but sun's warm
and the leaves of the beech,
maple, slur in the slight wind.
The long orange slide
ripples broadly down
to sand where Willy was
so young, so young!

—Berlin, June 7, 1987

Love

Nothing is without place,
in mind, in physical apprehension—

or if "a dagger of the mind" is the purpose,
hold on to it for dear life, or else kill somebody.

Just when I thought I had it made, I lost it.
Just when I knew what to do, I was an old man.

You hear that bird sing in the tree there,
you know still what a tree is?

Love is a place, not a person, love is
a weather of time, a convenience to absent sorrows.

But talk is the cheapest of all, means what it wants to,
 waits up for no one, always goes home alone.

For Neil Williams

Pieces you were always at
small place of the pardon
everything begun again it
thinks on its own behalf—

I loved you driving driving
space you made out of the heart
colors of obliterating pleasure
rock sun struck flat of water—

You said, like, teen age kid come
to LA to see the ocean, you
walked down street, thought it
was a hill, the Pacific—And on and on.

Places

Tidy, specific—
my head
or yours.

Sudden Sea

Watch wading kid
circa six plus, cropped
flaxen head, collar
of orange life jacket,
blue shorts just
at water's edge—
Smell sudden sea.

Take

Head's ventricles fast
action heard now past
gain up get in see that
rapid movement gets it
done like that wants more
time or money got your
person by the hand eats
thinks and sleeps feats
of amazing grace face off
fashion feels just fine
it's a dumb con line run
no fun get the mon in time
hon take the money and run.

The Times

If they had something
to worry about these
people wouldn't sit there
thinking about what

doesn't even exist they
would take each day as it
comes and thank their
lucky stars they had

enough to eat it says here
it reflects the hopeless
times make what isn't
the case all that is.

Was

Say Mr. Snowman *can
play a song for me*

yes *you*

Window

Sometimes it seems just
a push would get you over
the rooftops and out into air

it feels has nothing but
space to give you. This
riding high was made for serious

people who want to live but
can't. Just a push and you're up there,
out, and free as the birds.

Places *was designed by Mike Boughn
and set in ITC Garamond at
shuffaloff press.
500 copies were printed
of which 50 are numbered, hand-sewn,
and signed by the author and the artist.*

Shuffaloff press